Unleashing Influence: Harnessing Neurolinguistic Programming for Sales and Marketing Success

By Rex Morton

Copyright Page

Published by Omniterra Media Inc

First Edition

Visit the author's website at www.rexmorton.com

For information regarding special discounts for bulk purchases, please contact Rex Morton @ Rex@rexmorton.com.

Disclaimer

This book is intended to provide information about the fields of Neuro-Linguistic Programming (NLP) and Cognitive Behavioural Therapy (CBT) and their potential integration. While the author has made every effort to ensure that the information was correct at the time of publication, the author does not assume and hereby disclaims any liability to any party for any loss, damage, or disruption caused by errors or omissions, whether such errors or omissions result from negligence, accident, or any other cause.

The contents of this book should not be used as a substitute for professional advice, diagnosis, or treatment. The reader should always consult with a qualified healthcare provider about any mental health concerns or conditions. Never disregard professional psychological or medical advice or delay in seeking it because of something you have read in this book.

The views expressed in this work are solely those of the author and do not necessarily reflect the views of the publisher, and the publisher hereby disclaims any responsibility for them.

The inclusion of websites, links, or references to other resources does not mean that the author or the publisher endorses the information the organization or website may provide or recommendations it might make. Furthermore, the author does not guarantee the accuracy of the information these resources provide.

The use of any information provided in this book is solely at your own risk.

Introduction:

Neuro-Linguistic Programming (NLP) is a powerful methodology that encompasses a set of core principles and techniques for understanding human Behaviour and improving communication. In the realm of sales and marketing, where effective communication and influencing decision-making are paramount, NLP has emerged as a valuable tool. This comprehensive guide explores the science behind NLP, its role in communication, rapport building, decision influencing, overcoming objections and resistance, as well as its applications in marketing and sales strategies.

Understanding the intricate relationship between the brain, language, and behavioral patterns (programming) is the basis of NLP. NLP endeavors to discover successful strategies and techniques by analyzing the cognitive processes, linguistic patterns, and subjective experiences of individuals. Through the lens of NLP, sales and marketing professionals gain an understanding of the underlying factors that drive human behavior and learn how to tailor their approaches for optimal results.

The importance of effective communication cannot be overstated in the world of sales and marketing. NLP provides a framework for understanding how communication styles, language patterns, and non-verbal cues influence the way messages are received and interpreted. By employing NLP techniques such as mirroring, pacing, and leading, professionals can establish rapport, gain trust, and deliver their messages in a persuasive manner. This guide presents case studies that demonstrate the impact of NLP on communication effectiveness in real-world sales and marketing scenarios.

Building rapport is a fundamental aspect of successful sales and marketing endeavors. NLP offers a range of techniques for establishing rapport, including matching and mirroring, using similar language, and understanding sensory preferences. By aligning with the communication and Behavioural patterns of their prospects or customers, sales and marketing professionals can foster connections and create a conducive environment for mutual understanding and cooperation. The guide examines case studies that showcase the power of NLP in building rapport and forging meaningful relationships.

Influencing decision-making is a key objective in sales and marketing. NLP equips professionals with techniques to shape perceptions, frame information, and anchor positive associations. By understanding the cognitive processes underlying decision-making, practitioners can leverage NLP strategies to effectively guide prospects and customers towards desired outcomes. Through the exploration of case studies, this guide illustrates how NLP can influence decisions and drive successful sales and marketing campaigns.

Objections and resistance are common hurdles in sales and marketing. NLP provides practitioners with tools to overcome objections by reframing perspectives, utilizing presuppositions, and leveraging effective communication techniques. By addressing objections and resistance through an NLP lens, professionals can transform challenges into opportunities for persuasion and negotiation. The guide presents case studies that exemplify how NLP can overcome objections and resistance, leading to successful outcomes.

Beyond individual sales and marketing efforts, NLP also finds application in broader marketing and sales strategies. By incorporating NLP principles, companies can design campaigns that resonate with their target audience, evoke desired emotions, and effectively convey their brand messages. This guide explores successful marketing campaigns that have employed NLP strategies, shedding light on their effectiveness and impact.

Similarly, NLP can be integrated into sales strategies to enhance customer engagement, improve sales techniques, and boost conversion rates. The guide delves into case studies that highlight the implementation of NLP in successful sales strategies, providing valuable insights and inspiration for professionals seeking to elevate their sales performance.

While NLP offers powerful tools and techniques, it is essential to consider its limitations and ethical considerations. This guide examines the limitations of NLP and emphasizes the importance of ethical practices when using NLP in sales and marketing contexts. It underscores the significance of maintaining integrity, respect, and consent when employing NLP techniques.

The future of NLP in sales and marketing holds exciting possibilities. This guide explores current trends in NLP and its integration with sales and marketing strategies, offering predictions

Core principles and techniques of Neuro-Linguistic Programming (NLP):

Neuro-Linguistic Programming (NLP) encompasses a set of core principles and techniques that aim to understand human Behaviour, improve communication, and facilitate personal and professional development. Developed in the 1970s by Richard Bandler and John Grinder, NLP is based on the belief that by studying successful patterns of Behaviour, individuals can learn and replicate those patterns to achieve their desired outcomes.

The core principles of NLP revolve around three key components: neurology, language, and programming. The neurology aspect emphasizes that human Behaviour is influenced by the sensory experiences and neurological processes within an individual's mind. Language refers to the way we use words and non-verbal communication to create meaning and interact with others. Programming suggests that individuals can reprogram their thoughts, emotions, and Behaviours by understanding and modifying their internal processes.

To achieve effective communication and personal growth, NLP employs a range of techniques. These techniques include:

Rapport Building: Building rapport is crucial for establishing trust, understanding, and cooperation. NLP techniques such as matching and mirroring, where one person aligns their body language, vocal tone, and language patterns with another, can help create a sense of connection and mutual understanding.

Sensory Acuity: NLP emphasizes the importance of developing sensory acuity to observe and interpret non-verbal cues and subtle changes in Behaviour. By sharpening their sensory perception, practitioners can gain valuable insights into the thoughts, feelings, and preferences of others.

Anchoring: Anchoring is the process of associating a particular stimulus, such as a touch or a word, with a specific affective state. By creating positive anchors, individuals are able to access desired emotional states at will, enabling them to function optimally in a variety of circumstances.

Reframing: Reframing is the process of altering the meaning or context of a situation in order to alter an individual's perception and emotional reaction. By reframing a difficulty as an opportunity or a setback as a learning experience, individuals can transform their mindset and approach in order to achieve positive results.

Language Patterns: NLP pays careful attention to language patterns and the impact they have on communication. Techniques such as presuppositions, which involve embedding assumptions into statements, and the Milton Model, a set of language patterns designed to influence and persuade, are used to enhance communication effectiveness.

Overview of Sales and Marketing Principles:

Sales and marketing principles form the foundation of successful business strategies aimed at attracting customers, promoting products or services, and driving revenue growth. These principles encompass various fundamental concepts and practices that guide professionals in effectively reaching and engaging their target audience. Some key principles include:

Target Market Analysis: Understanding the needs, preferences, and Behaviours of the target market is essential for developing tailored marketing strategies. By conducting market research and analyzing demographic, psychographic, and Behavioural data, businesses can identify their ideal customer profiles and create targeted campaigns.

Value Proposition: Articulating a compelling value proposition is crucial in sales and marketing. Businesses must clearly communicate the unique benefits and value their products or services offer to customers. A strong value proposition differentiates a company from its competitors and convinces prospects of the benefits they will gain by choosing the business's offerings.

Branding: Building a strong brand identity helps establish trust, recognition, and loyalty among customers. Effective branding involves creating a distinct brand image, positioning the brand in the market, and consistently delivering on the brand promise. Branding plays a vital role in shaping customer perceptions and influencing purchasing decisions.

Marketing Mix: The marketing mix consists of the four Ps: product, price, place, and promotion. This principle involves strategically designing and managing these elements to meet customer needs, maximize profitability, and achieve marketing objectives. The right product, pricing strategy, distribution channels, and promotional tactics contribute to the success of marketing efforts.

The importance of communication in sales and marketing:

Communication lies at the heart of sales and marketing endeavors. Effective communication is essential for conveying messages, building relationships, understanding customer needs, and persuading prospects to take desired actions. Here are some reasons why communication is vital in sales and marketing:

Conveying Information: Sales and marketing professionals need to effectively communicate the features, benefits, and value of their products or services to customers. Clear and concise communication helps prospects understand how a particular offering can address their needs or solve their problems.

Relationship Building: Building relationships with prospects and customers is crucial for long-term success. Strong communication skills enable sales and marketing professionals to establish rapport, gain trust, and develop meaningful connections. Effective communication fosters positive interactions, enhances customer satisfaction, and encourages repeat business.

Persuasion and Influence: Persuasive communication is a powerful tool in sales and marketing. By employing persuasive techniques and crafting compelling messages, professionals can influence customer perceptions, change attitudes, and motivate prospects to make purchasing decisions.

Understanding Customer Needs: Effective communication allows professionals to actively listen to customers, ask relevant questions, and understand their unique needs and preferences. This understanding helps tailor marketing strategies, customize offerings, and provide personalized solutions that resonate with customers.

How Neuro-Linguistic Programming Affects Communication:

Neuro-Linguistic Programming (NLP) has a profound impact on communication by providing individuals with tools and techniques to enhance their ability to connect, understand, and influence others. Here are some ways in which NLP affects communication:

Increased Rapport: NLP techniques contribute to building rapport, which is the foundation of effective communication. Techniques like mirroring, where one person subtly matches the body language, gestures, and speech patterns of another, establish a sense of familiarity and connection. Pacing, another NLP technique, involves matching the tempo and style of communication to create harmony and rapport with the other person.

Enhanced Understanding: NLP emphasizes the importance of sensory acuity and active listening. By developing these skills, individuals can better interpret verbal and non-verbal cues, allowing for a deeper understanding of the other person's thoughts, feelings, and intentions. This heightened understanding enables more meaningful and effective communication.

Flexibility in Communication Styles: NLP recognizes that individuals have different communication preferences. By understanding and adapting to the preferred sensory modalities (visual, auditory, kinesthetic) of others, communicators can tailor their language and delivery to resonate with the listener. This flexibility facilitates better communication and ensures the message is received and understood in a way that aligns with the listener s communication style.

Influence and Persuasion: NLP equips individuals with techniques for influencing and persuading others. For example, leading involves subtly guiding the conversation and influencing the direction of thoughts and emotions. The use of language patterns, such as embedded commands or presuppositions, can also influence the listener's subconscious mind and shape their perceptions and responses.

Techniques for effective communication using Neuro-Linguistic Programming:

Neuro-Linguistic Programming offers a range of techniques to enhance communication effectiveness. Here are some key techniques used in NLP:

Mirroring: Mirroring involves subtly matching the body language, gestures, and speech patterns of the other person. This technique creates a sense of familiarity and rapport, making the other person more receptive to communication.

Pacing and Leading: Pacing involves matching the tempo, rhythm, and language style of the other person. This establishes rapport and builds a connection. Leading occurs when the communicator gradually leads the conversation in a desired direction, guiding the thoughts and emotions of the other person.

Sensory-Based Language: NLP encourages the use of sensory-based language to enhance communication impact. By incorporating sensory words and vivid descriptions, communicators can engage the listener's imagination and create a more immersive experience.

Active Listening: NLP emphasizes active listening, which involves giving full attention to the speaker and observing verbal and non-verbal cues. Active listening enables the communicator to understand the underlying meaning, emotions, and needs of the other person, facilitating more effective and empathetic communication.

Language Patterns: NLP utilizes various language patterns to influence and persuade. These patterns include embedded commands, where suggestions are subtly embedded within sentences, and presuppositions, which involve embedding assumptions or statements that presuppose a certain belief or outcome.

Case studies of effective Neuro-Linguistic Programming communication in sales and marketing:

Several case studies demonstrate the effectiveness of NLP communication techniques in sales and marketing contexts. Here are a few examples:

Case Study 1: In a sales setting, a sales representative uses mirroring and pacing techniques to establish rapport with a prospective client. By subtly matching the client's body language, speech patterns, and pace of speech, the sales representative creates a sense of familiarity and connection. This rapport-building technique increases the client's trust and receptiveness to the sales pitch, leading to a higher likelihood of closing the sale.

Case Study 2: In a marketing campaign, a company utilizes sensory-based language and vivid imagery in their messaging. By appealing to the senses and creating a multisensory experience through their marketing materials, the company captures the attention and engages the target audience on a deeper level. This NLP technique enhances the effectiveness of the campaign and strengthens the brand's connection with the audience.

Case Study 3: In a negotiation scenario, a skilled negotiator applies pacing and leading techniques to guide the conversation and influence the outcome. By initially matching the communication style and preferences of the other party, the negotiator establishes rapport and builds trust. Gradually, the negotiator leads the conversation towards their desired objectives, using language patterns and persuasive techniques to shape the negotiation process in their favor.

These case studies highlight the tangible benefits of incorporating NLP communication techniques in sales and marketing. By employing NLP principles and techniques, professionals can enhance their ability to connect with their audience, influence decisions, and achieve desired outcomes. NLP offers a valuable set of tools for effective communication in sales and marketing contexts.

Understanding Objections and Resistance in Sales and Marketing:

Objections and resistance are common challenges faced in sales and marketing efforts. When prospects or customers express objections or resistance, it means they have concerns, doubts, or hesitations that need to be addressed before they can proceed with a purchase or engagement. Understanding objections and resistance is crucial in sales and marketing for the following reasons:

Identifying Needs: Objections and resistance often provide valuable insights into the needs, preferences, and concerns of prospects or customers. By understanding the underlying reasons for objections, sales and marketing professionals can tailor their approach and offerings to better meet the needs of the Customer.

Building Trust: Effectively addressing objections and resistance helps to develop prospects' and customers' trust and credibility. When professionals take the time to attend, comprehend, and address objections, they demonstrate their dedication to customer satisfaction and willingness to address concerns. This increases the likelihood of a successful outcome and fosters trust.

Overcoming Barriers: Objections and resistance act as barriers to closing a sale or achieving a desired outcome. By effectively handling objections and overcoming resistance, professionals can remove these barriers and progress towards a positive decision or action. This requires employing effective communication and persuasion techniques.

Neuro-Linguistic Programming techniques for overcoming objections and resistance:

Neuro-Linguistic Programming (NLP) provides techniques that can be applied to overcome objections and resistance in sales and marketing. Here are some NLP techniques commonly used for this purpose:

Reframing: Reframing involves shifting the perspective or context of an objection or resistance. By helping the prospect or Customer see the objection in a different light, professionals can change their perception and open up new possibilities. Reframing can involve highlighting different benefits, presenting alternative viewpoints, or focusing on positive outcomes.

Presuppositions: NLP utilizes presuppositions, which are statements that assume certain beliefs or conditions to be true. By strategically using presuppositions in responses to objections or resistance, professionals can redirect the focus and influence the prospect's or Customer's thinking. This helps move the conversation forward and address the objection from a different angle.

Meta-Model Questions: The Meta-Model is a set of linguistic patterns in NLP that allows professionals to uncover and clarify the underlying meaning behind objections or resistance. By asking specific Meta-Model questions, professionals can gather more information, challenge assumptions, and facilitate deeper understanding. This helps to address objections more effectively.

Anchoring Positive States: NLP techniques involving anchoring can be used to create positive emotional states and associations during objection handling. By using anchors that elicit positive emotions or memories, professionals can shift the prospect's or Customer's state of mind, reducing resistance and increasing receptiveness to their message.

Case studies of overcoming objections and resistance using Neuro-Linguistic Programming:

Real-world case studies demonstrate the effectiveness of NLP techniques in overcoming objections and resistance in sales and marketing. Here are a few examples:

Case Study 1: During a sales presentation, a prospect expresses an objection related to price. The sales professional utilizes reframing techniques by highlighting the long-term value and return on investment the product or service can provide. By reframing the objection from a cost perspective to a value perspective, the sales professional addresses the objection and successfully convinces the prospect of the worthiness of the investment.

Case Study 2: In a customer service interaction, a customer expresses resistance to upgrading their service plan. The customer service representative uses presuppositions by assuming that the Customer agrees with certain positive aspects of the upgrade. By framing their responses with presuppositions, the representative redirects the focus and subtly guides the Customer towards considering the benefits of the upgrade. This overcomes the resistance and leads to a positive outcome where the Customer agrees to upgrade their service plan.

Case Study 3: In a marketing campaign, potential customers express objections regarding the quality and reliability of a product. The marketing team utilizes Meta-Model questions to uncover the specific concerns and gather more information. By asking questions to clarify the objections and address any misconceptions, the team is able to provide accurate information, alleviate concerns, and effectively overcome the objections. This leads to an increase in customer trust and a higher likelihood of conversion.

These case studies highlight how NLP techniques can be applied to overcome objections and resistance in sales and marketing. By utilizing reframing, presuppositions, Meta-Model questions, and other NLP strategies, professionals can effectively address objections, challenge assumptions, and shift perspectives. This enables them to overcome resistance and guide prospects or customers towards a positive decision or action.

Neuro-Linguistic Programming techniques provide valuable tools for handling objections and resistance, ultimately increasing the chances of successful sales and marketing outcomes. By integrating NLP into objection handling strategies, professionals can build stronger customer relationships, improve customer satisfaction, and achieve their sales and marketing goals.

Neuro-Linguistic Programming For Marketing Strategies

Neuro-Linguistic Programming (NLP) offers valuable insights and techniques that can significantly enhance marketing strategies. By understanding the psychology of consumers and employing effective communication techniques, NLP can optimize marketing campaigns for better engagement, persuasion, and customer satisfaction. Here's how NLP can be applied in marketing strategies:

Targeted Communication: NLP emphasizes the importance of understanding and adapting to the preferred communication styles, sensory modalities, and language patterns of the target audience. By tailoring marketing messages to resonate with the audience's preferences, marketers can increase the effectiveness of their communication and enhance audience engagement.

Persuasive Language: NLP provides techniques for using persuasive language patterns, such as embedded commands, presuppositions, and metaphors, to influence and motivate the audience. By strategically incorporating these language patterns in marketing materials, marketers can enhance the persuasive impact of their messaging and encourage desired customer Behaviours.

Building Rapport: Building rapport with the target audience is crucial for establishing trust and connection. NLP techniques like mirroring, matching, and pacing can help marketers create rapport by aligning their communication style with that of the audience. This fosters a sense of familiarity and understanding, enhancing the audience's receptiveness to the marketing message.

Understanding Consumer Needs: NLP techniques, such as active listening and sensory acuity, enable marketers to better understand the needs, desires, and pain points of the target audience. By actively listening to customer feedback and observing non-verbal cues, marketers can gain valuable insights that inform the development of more targeted and impactful marketing strategies.

Effective Storytelling: NLP emphasizes the power of storytelling in marketing. By utilizing NLP techniques like sensory-rich language, visual imagery, and engaging narratives, marketers can create compelling stories that captivate the audience's attention, evoke emotions, and establish a strong connection with the brand or product.

Case studies of successful marketing campaigns that used Neuro-Linguistic Programming:

Several successful marketing campaigns have leveraged NEURO-LINGUISTIC PROGRAMMING techniques to achieve outstanding results. Here are a few examples:

Case Study 1: A skincare brand utilized NLP techniques in their marketing campaign. By employing persuasive language patterns, such as presuppositions and embedded commands, in their messaging, they influenced the audience's perception of their products. The campaign's focus on sensory-rich language and vivid imagery created an immersive experience that appealed to the audience's emotions. This led to a rise in brand engagement, a rise in conversion rates, and an increase in consumer loyalty.

Case Study 2: An online retailer incorporated NLP principles into their email marketing strategy. They tailored their communication by segmenting their email list based on the sensory modalities preferred by the audience (visual, auditory, kinesthetic). By delivering personalized messages that aligned with each segment's communication style, they achieved higher open and click-through rates. The implementation of mirroring and pacing techniques in email copy enhanced rapport and fostered a stronger connection with the audience.

Case Study 3: An automobile manufacturer implemented NLP techniques in their television commercials. By using metaphors and storytelling techniques, they created emotional connections between the audience and their brand. The commercials showcased captivating narratives that resonated with the audience's aspirations and desires. This approach resulted in increased brand affinity, improved brand perception, and higher purchase intent among the target audience.

These case studies illustrate the successful application of NEURO-LINGUISTIC PROGRAMMING in marketing campaigns. By incorporating NLP techniques, marketers can enhance audience engagement, influence decision-making processes, and create more meaningful and effective connections with their target audience. NLP offers valuable tools for understanding consumer psychology, tailoring communication, and optimizing marketing strategies for better results.

NEURO-LINGUISTIC PROGRAMMING enables marketers to tap into the subconscious factors that influence consumer Behaviour. By understanding the language, communication styles, and preferences of their target audience, marketers can create more impactful and persuasive marketing campaigns. The application of NLP techniques such as targeted communication, persuasive language, rapport-building, understanding consumer needs, and effective storytelling can greatly enhance marketing strategies.

By utilizing NLP principles, marketers can connect with their audience on a deeper level, evoke emotions, and influence their perception of the brand or product. This results in an increase in consumer engagement, brand loyalty, and conversion rates.

Incorporating NLP techniques into marketing strategies is not limited to a specific industry or business size. The flexibility of NLP allows marketers to adapt and tailor their approaches to various target audiences and marketing channels.

The success of NLP in marketing campaigns can be seen through the measurable outcomes achieved by companies that have implemented these techniques. By applying NLP principles and techniques, marketers have reported increased customer engagement, improved brand perception, higher conversion rates, and enhanced customer loyalty.

It is important to note that the effectiveness of NLP techniques in marketing strategies relies on ethical implementation.

Marketers should always prioritize transparency, respect customer boundaries, and ensure that their marketing efforts align with ethical standards.

Overall, the integration of Neuro-Linguistic Programming in marketing strategies offers a powerful framework for understanding and influencing consumer Behaviour. By utilizing NLP techniques, marketers can create more persuasive campaigns that resonate with their target audience, increase engagement, and ultimately help them achieve their marketing objectives.

Neuro-Linguistic Programming For Sales Strategies

Neuro-Linguistic Programming (NLP) offers valuable techniques and principles that can significantly enhance sales strategies. By understanding the psychology of buyers and employing effective communication strategies, NLP can optimize the sales process for improved engagement, persuasion, and closing rates. Here's how NLP can be applied in sales strategies:

Building Rapport: NLP techniques play a crucial role in building rapport with potential customers. Techniques like mirroring, matching, and pacing enable sales professionals to establish a connection and create a sense of familiarity with the buyer. This helps build trust, strengthen relationships, and increase the chances of a successful sale.

Effective Communication: NLP provides tools for effective communication in sales. Techniques such as active listening, sensory acuity, and language patterns allow sales professionals to better understand and respond to the needs, concerns, and preferences of buyers. By adapting their communication style and language to match the buyer's preferred sensory modality, sales professionals can establish better rapport and convey information more effectively.

Overcoming Objections: NLP offers techniques to address and overcome objections effectively. Techniques like reframing enable sales professionals to shift the buyer's perspective and present the product or service in a more favorable light. NLP also provides strategies for understanding the underlying meaning behind objections and addressing them in a way that aligns with the buyer's values and goals.

Influencing Decision-Making: NLP techniques can be applied to influence the decision-making process of buyers. By utilizing techniques such as anchoring, sales professionals can associate positive emotions or experiences with their product or service. This can influence the buyer's perception and increase their likelihood of making a favorable decision.

Effective Closing Techniques: NLP offers strategies for effective closing in sales. Techniques like presuppositions and embedded commands can be used to guide the buyer towards taking the desired action. NLP also provides tools for managing objections and resistance during the closing phase, allowing sales professionals to address concerns and overcome barriers to a successful sale.

Case studies of successful sales strategies that used Neuro-Linguistic Programming:

Several case studies demonstrate the success of integrating Neuro-Linguistic Programming techniques into sales strategies. Here are a few examples:

Case Study 1: A sales team in the insurance industry applied NLP techniques during sales presentations. By utilizing mirroring and matching techniques, they built rapport with potential clients and established a sense of trust. Through effective communication and active listening, they were able to understand the specific needs and concerns of each client. This enabled them to address objections, tailor their messaging, and ultimately close more sales.

Case Study 2: A software company implemented NLP techniques in their sales process. By utilizing reframing techniques, they effectively addressed objections related to cost and implementation. They reframed the discussion to focus on the long-term benefits and return on investment for the client. By using persuasive language patterns and incorporating customer testimonials, they successfully influenced the buyer's decision-making process and achieved higher conversion rates.

Case Study 3: A sales team in the automotive industry integrated NLP techniques into their closing strategies. By utilizing anchoring techniques, they associated positive emotions and experiences with test drives and the overall car ownership experience. This influenced the buyer's perception and increased their desire to take the final step in purchasing the vehicle. The implementation of embedded commands and effective objection-handling techniques further enhanced the closing process, resulting in improved sales performance.

These case studies demonstrate the effectiveness of NEURO-LINGUISTIC PROGRAMMING techniques in sales strategies. By integrating NLP principles and techniques, sales professionals can enhance their communication, build rapport, address objections, influence decision-making, and improve their overall sales performance. NEURO-LINGUISTIC PROGRAMMING provides a powerful framework for understanding and influencing buyer Behaviour, enabling sales professionals to connect with customers on a deeper level and guide them towards making favorable purchasing decisions.

By applying NLP techniques, sales teams have reported increased success in building rapport, addressing objections, influencing decision-making, and ultimately closing more sales. The ability to adapt communication styles, actively listen, reframe objections, and use persuasive language patterns empowers sales professionals to effectively engage with customers and overcome challenges throughout the sales process.

It's important to note that the successful implementation of Neuro-Linguistic Programming in sales strategies requires ethical considerations. Sales professionals should always prioritize transparency, honesty, and respect for the buyer's needs and preferences. NLP techniques should be used responsibly, with the goal of creating mutually beneficial outcomes.

Overall, Neuro-Linguistic Programming offers valuable tools and techniques for enhancing sales strategies. By leveraging NLP principles, sales professionals can optimize their communication, build stronger relationships with customers, and increase their effectiveness in closing sales. Integrating NLP into sales strategies can lead to improved sales performance, customer satisfaction, and business growth.

Limitations and Ethical Considerations of Neuro-Linguistic Programming in Sales and Marketing:

Neuro-Linguistic Programming (NLP) provides techniques and principles that can improve sales and marketing techniques. Nonetheless, it is essential to acknowledge and resolve the limitations and ethical concerns associated with its application. Understanding these factors ensures responsible and ethical use of NLP in sales and marketing contexts. Here's a discussion of the limitations and the importance of ethical considerations:

Limitations of Neuro-Linguistic Programming:

Individual Variability: NLP techniques may not yield identical results for each individual. An individual's response to NLP techniques can be influenced by cultural background, personal beliefs, and past experiences. It is essential to recognize that NLP techniques may not be universally effective and that they must be tailored to the specific requirements and preferences of the intended audience.

Ethical Concerns: While NLP can be a powerful tool, its effectiveness should never compromise ethical standards. It is crucial to use NLP techniques responsibly and avoid manipulation or coercion. Ethical concerns arise when NLP techniques are used to deceive or exploit individuals, misrepresent products or services, or infringe upon personal boundaries. Practitioners should always prioritize transparency, respect, and the well-being of customers.

The Importance of Ethical Considerations when using Neuro-Linguistic Programming in Sales and Marketing:

Trust and Long-Term Relationships: Ethical considerations are vital in sales and marketing because they contribute to building trust and fostering long-term relationships with customers. When customers perceive sales and marketing efforts as honest, transparent, and respectful, they are more likely to develop trust and loyalty towards the brand. Ethical conduct ensures that customers feel valued, leading to positive brand perceptions and increased customer satisfaction.

Customer Well-Being: Ethical considerations prioritize the well-being and best interests of customers. Sales and marketing professionals have a responsibility to provide accurate information, avoid misleading claims, and genuinely meet customer needs. By adhering to ethical standards, professionals ensure that customers make informed decisions and are not coerced or manipulated into purchasing products or services that do not align with their best interests.

Reputation and Brand Image: Unethical practices can have severe consequences for a company's reputation and brand image. Negative experiences or deceptive tactics can damage the trust and credibility that have been established with customers over time. Ethical conduct in sales and marketing contributes to a positive brand image, strengthens brand reputation, and builds a foundation of trust among customers and stakeholders.

Legal Compliance: Ethical considerations align with legal requirements and regulations in sales and marketing. It is crucial to ensure that NLP techniques and practices comply with applicable laws, industry standards, and consumer protection regulations. Violating legal obligations can result in legal consequences, reputational damage, and loss of customer trust.

By integrating ethical considerations into the use of NLP techniques, sales and marketing professionals can cultivate positive relationships, maintain brand integrity, and promote customer satisfaction. Ethical conduct ensures that NLP techniques are applied responsibly and with respect for the rights and well-being of customers.

It is important for organizations to provide proper training and guidance to sales and marketing teams on the ethical use of NLP techniques. By fostering a culture of ethical decision-making and providing clear guidelines, companies can ensure that NLP is implemented responsibly and in alignment with ethical standards, benefiting both the business and its customers.

Current Trends in Neuro-Linguistic Programming and Sales and Marketing:

Neuro-Linguistic Programming (NLP) continues to evolve and find new applications in sales and marketing. Here are some current trends in the intersection of NLP and sales and marketing:

Personalization and Customization: Personalization is a significant trend in sales and marketing, and NLP techniques can contribute to this by enabling professionals to tailor their communication and messaging to individual customers. By understanding customer preferences, communication styles, and needs, sales and marketing professionals can create personalized experiences that resonate with customers on a deeper level, leading to increased engagement and conversion rates.

Emotional Intelligence and Empathy: Emotional intelligence and empathy are becoming increasingly important in sales and marketing. NLP techniques help professionals develop these skills by enhancing their ability to understand and connect with customers at an emotional level. By leveraging NLP techniques such as rapport-building, active listening, and empathetic communication, professionals can create a more empathetic and customer-centric sales and marketing approach.

Neuro-marketing: Neuro-marketing is a growing field that combines neuroscience with marketing strategies. NLP techniques play a significant role in understanding consumer Behaviour, decision-making processes, and influencing buyer psychology. By leveraging NLP principles and techniques, marketers can gain insights into consumer motivations, preferences, and cognitive processes, allowing them to develop more effective marketing strategies and campaigns.

Predictions for the future of Neuro-Linguistic Programming in sales and marketing:

Enhanced Customer Experience: The future of NLP in sales and marketing is likely to focus on enhancing the customer experience. As technology advances, NLP can be integrated into various customer touchpoints, enabling personalized interactions, intuitive conversational interfaces, and AI-powered customer support. NLP-powered chatbots and virtual assistants may become more sophisticated in understanding and responding to customer needs, delivering highly tailored experiences.

Multi-channel Communication: The future of NLP in sales and marketing will likely involve seamless integration across multiple communication channels. NLP techniques can be applied to optimize communication in various formats, including voice assistants, messaging apps, social media, and augmented reality/virtual reality experiences. This will enable marketers to deliver consistent and personalized messaging across diverse platforms, creating a cohesive customer journey.

Data-Driven Insights: As customer data becomes more readily available, the future of NLP in sales and marketing will entail leveraging data-driven insights. The combination of NLP techniques with data analytics and machine learning enables sales and marketing professionals to gain a deeper understanding of consumer behavior, preferences, and sentiment. This will enable more precise targeting, personalized communication, and improved decision-making.

Ethical and Transparent Use: As NLP continues to advance in sales and marketing, the importance of ethical and transparent use will become even more pronounced. Companies will need to prioritize responsible and ethical application of NLP techniques, ensuring that customer privacy is respected, consent is obtained, and transparent communication is maintained. Ethical considerations will play a crucial role in shaping the future of NLP in sales and marketing.

Overall, the future of NLP in sales and marketing holds immense potential for improving customer engagement, personalization, and decision-making. By leveraging the power of NLP techniques and combining them with emerging technologies, organizations can create more effective sales and marketing strategies that align with customer expectations and preferences.

Conclusion

In conclusion, Neuro-Linguistic Programming (NLP) offers valuable principles and techniques that can significantly enhance sales and marketing strategies. By understanding the psychology of buyers, adapting communication styles, and leveraging persuasive language patterns, professionals can create more impactful and personalized interactions with customers. NLP empowers sales and marketing teams to build rapport, address objections, influence decision-making, and ultimately achieve better results.

However, it is important to acknowledge the limitations of NLP and ensure ethical considerations are prioritized. NLP techniques may not have universal effectiveness, and individual variability should be taken into account. Ethical considerations are crucial in maintaining trust, building long-term relationships, and prioritizing customer well-being. By adhering to ethical standards, companies can safeguard their reputation, establish positive brand images, and comply with legal requirements.

Current trends in NLP and sales and marketing highlight the importance of personalization, emotional intelligence, and neuro-marketing. The future of NLP in sales and marketing predicts enhanced customer experiences, multi-channel communication, data-driven insights, and a focus on ethical and transparent use. By embracing these trends and leveraging the power of N_P techniques, organizations can create tailored experiences, optimize customer engagement, and stay ahead in the evolving landscape of sales and marketing.

In summary, the integration of NLP into sales and marketing strategies offers a valuable framework for understanding consumer Eehaviour, enhancing communication, and influencing decision-making. By combining NLP principles with ethical considerations and emerging technologies, organizations can unlock new opportunities, deliver exceptional customer experiences, and achieve their sales and marketing objectives in a responsible and customer-centric manner.

About the Author

Rex Morton is a renowned author and researcher in the United Kingdom with a passionate interest in the human mind, specifically in Cognitive Behavioural Therapy (CBT) and Neuro-Linguistic Programming (NLP).

Morton has spent a considerable portion of his professional life diving deep into the theories and principles that form the backbone of these two compelling fields. His fascination with NLP led him to complete an extensive certification program, solidifying his understanding of this innovative approach to understanding human Behaviour.

Although Morton does not have clinical experience, his intense curiosity and dedication to studying these subjects have made him a respected figure in the field. He has thoroughly researched the integration of NLP techniques into CBT, offering fresh perspectives and insights into how these two methodologies can complement each other to enhance understanding of human cognition and Behaviour.

As an author, Morton has successfully communicated his knowledge and passion to a broader audience, making complex psychological theories accessible to professionals and interested laypersons. His writing is characterized by a clear, engaging style and a focus on the practical application of theories, making them relevant to everyday life.

In his personal life, Morton is an ardent lover of the natural world, often spending his free time exploring the British countryside. His passion for landscape photography allows him to capture and share the beauty of these excursions. Despite his accomplishments, Morton is known for his humility and eagerness to continue learning. His work continues to inspire those interested in the intricate workings of the human mind and the exciting possibilities presented by the integration of NLP and CBT.

If you've found the content of this book enlightening and wish to continue your journey of understanding the human mind, I warmly invite you to visit my website at www.rexmorton.com. The website serves as a hub of knowledge where I share my latest findings, thoughts, and insights on the integration of NLP and CBT.

I also encourage you to subscribe to the newsletter available on the website. By subscribing, you'll receive regular updates on a range of topics, from detailed discussions on specific NLP techniques and their application in CBT, to the latest research in the field.

The newsletter is also the first place I'll share news of upcoming releases. Whether it's the announcement of a new book, the launch of an online course, newsletter subscribers will be the first to know. This is a great opportunity to continue learning directly from me, deepening your understanding of NLP and CBT, and enhancing your skills in applying these techniques in your own life or professional practice.

I'm looking forward to sharing this journey with you.

www.ingramcontent.com/pod-product-compliance
Lightning Source LLC
Chambersburg PA
CBHW062301290526
45794CB00006B/2654